Heaven Waits

Written and published by
Josh Bruckerhoff

Contents

A God Who is now

We've been wrong about judgment

It won't always be this way

Is that all you've got?

Heaven Waits

A God Who is now

I can't wait to talk about this.

It's about Heaven.

And how we may have it wrong.

Listen to Maria Shriver's definition in her children's book *What's Heaven:*

> *"a beautiful place where you can sit on soft clouds and talk... If you're good throughout your life, then you get to go there... When your life is finished here on earth, God sends angels down to take you heaven to be with him."*

But listen to what N. T. Wright, one of my favorite authors, says about Heaven:

> *"Never at any point do the Gospels or Paul say Jesus has been raised, therefore we are we are all going to heaven. They all say, Jesus is raised,*

therefore the new creation has begun, and we have a job to do"

"It's more exciting than hanging around listening to nice music. In Revelation and Paul's letters we are told that God's people will actually be running the new world on God's behalf. The idea of our participation in the new creation goes back to Genesis, when humans are supposed to be running the Garden and looking after the animals. If you transpose that all the way through, it's a picture like the one that you get at the end of Revelation"

"If people think "my physical body doesn't matter very much," then who cares what I do with it? And if people think that our world, our cosmos, doesn't matter much, who cares what we do with that? Much of "traditional" Christianity gives the impression that God has these rather arbitrary rules about how you have to behave, and if you disobey them you go to hell, rather than to heaven. What the New Testament really says is God wants you to be a renewed human being helping him to renew his creation, and his resurrection was the opening bell. And when he returns to fulfil the plan, you won't be going up there to him,

> *he'll be coming down here"* - Interview with Time Magazine February 7th, 2008

Like I said, I'm very excited to dive into this.

A God Who is now

Application: What is God saying to me?

Heaven Waits

We've been wrong about judgment

I've wanted to write about this for a while, but before I do, let me mention something.

This book is not refuting the idea that Heaven exists. It isn't anti-Heaven. I believe in Heaven. But this isn't just a book about Heaven, however. It's a book about hope. It is a book about where, or who, or what we hope toward.

So let's begin.

Do you ever wonder why we buy stuff we don't need? Think about it. Look at any marketing campaign, and their message isn't really the product. What they are really trying to sell is hope. Hope that our lives can be better than they currently are. Their message: *You aren't as happy as you should be.* The same thing Satan told Eve in the garden.

But hope isn't a new thing.

I love the prophets. I think maybe it's because I'm a dork. And I think they were probably dorks too.

I mean think about it... Isaiah ran around naked to make a point *(thankfully, God hasn't called me to this ministry),* and Ezekiel lay on his side for over a year to make a point. I mean these guys are a bit weird, aren't they?

But what I love most about the prophets' writings is that it was God's raw judgment lined with hope. The prophets warn about how the Israelites will be oppressed, due to their worship of idols. But the prophets always mention hope. Hope in a day when things won't be this way. In a day there will be no more oppression. When evil wouldn't win. When God would take back His creation. Many Jews today use terms like *"Eden"* to describe what this will be like. This is the day when the Lord returns to His people, and makes everything right... when He makes things as they should be...

When the saints who have died will be resurrected.

They call this the Day of the Lord or the *Day of Judgment.*

In our church culture, "*Judgment*" has a negative connotation. But not to the Jews. Because they were the ones being oppressed, they were poor, they were mistreated. And the Day of Judgment is when they would finally become the people who God called them to be.

But they also called this day the Resurrection.

One of my favorite prophets is Isaiah. It is a remarkable book.

A few cliffnotes.

Isaiah talks about a trumpet sounding (27:13), comparing the Jews to a woman going through pains in childbirth (26:17), about how something new is coming out of it.

And it talks about the dead rising (26:19).

And the way Isaiah describes the Day of Judgment or Resurrection is a wedding (25:6), a time when Heaven comes to Earth, a time when things are going well, a time of celebration... where there will be wine.

I'd like end this chapter with a story.

Beware: this story could move you to tears.

> *My Night with Three Haitian Whores*
> by Tony Campolo
>
> One time when I was in Haiti, I checked into a modern hotel in the afternoon before I was to leave. There's only one Holiday Inn in that wreck of a country, and I stay overnight there to shower, shave, and get cleaned up so I'm fit for the plane ride home in the morning.
>
> After I'd gone down the block to get some dinner as I returned to the hotel entrance, 3 little girls intercepted me. I call them girls, because they couldn't have been more than 12 or 13. They had painted some lipstick on and were trying

to look sexy. But it's hard to look sexy when you're 13 and hungry.

The one in the middle boldly said "*Mister, for $10 dollars I'll do anything you want me to all night long.*"

And I cringed.

I looked at the one next to her and I said, "*How about you…can I have you for $10?*"

She said "*Oui.*"

I asked the third, "*What about you?*"

The third girl said in her broken English, "*Yes, you can have me for $10, too.*"

I said "*I've got $30…I want all three of you all night long. I'm in room 210, and I want you up there in a half hour.*"

Rushing up to the room, I called the concierge desk and asked "*I notice that you have videos for rent for the VCR's in the room, right? Send up every Disney video that you have."* Then I called room service: "*I want 4 huge dishes of chocolate ice cream. Please cover them with nuts, strawberry sauce, chocolate syrup, whipped cream, and cherries on top of each one. Make them big and beautiful. And I would like them up here in exactly a half hour."*

Right on time the little ladies knocked timidly on my door, and I ushered them in, where they sat down frightened on the edge of the bed. Shortly thereafter was another knock on the door and in came the videos and the ice cream…and these girls sat there wide-eyed, but still having no idea what was happening. So I put on *Finding Nemo*, and we ate the ice cream, and we started to laugh and joke and giggle, prompted by these strange images on the screen. When one video was done, we'd start another. I ordered up sandwich plates and lemonades at 11 o'clock. And we ate and watched cartoons and laughed some more.

By 2 AM, each of them had fallen asleep on the bed. As I sat there on the chair looking across at those 3 lovely, innocent whores, I thought *"Greater works shall you do because I go unto my Father."*

I didn't solve their problem. The next day they would be out on the streets again selling their little bodies. There would always be filthy johns around waiting to buy them. I didn't know enough Creole to tell them about Jesus, or to lead them to Him. Everything was the same…nothing had changed.

Except this: *for one night…just for one night, they were allowed to be little girls again.*

I choose to believe that the Kingdom of Heaven looks a bit more like this and a bit less like angels floating on clouds.

We’ve been wrong about judgment

Application: What is God saying to me?

Heaven Waits

It won’t always be this way

As mentioned previously, this isn't a book about heaven. But it is a book about hope. Because what we hope toward is what we live toward. And I don't think our hope should be in some far off place that has nothing to do with where we are today. So here we go.

Last chapter, I talked about the Day of Judgment and how it wasn't a bad thing to the Jews. And I talked about how the Day of the Lord is presented in the Bible as a wedding feast (Isaiah 25:6-8).

Interesting that Jesus's ministry starts with a wedding, isn't it? One thing I recently realized about the water into wine miracle: This represented Israel. This wedding that ran out of wine represented Israel. But Jesus steps in, His servants obey, and the best is saved for last.

And it happened on the third day.

The original readers got this, because what else happened on the third day? The resurrection.

Central to this kingdom of God, was a wedding. And Jesus begins His ministry at a wedding, a wedding that points to the resurrection.

So somehow the restoration of all things, the time when Christ sets up His Kingdom, when things are restored to the way they were first intended to be *(Eden)*... somehow this is all plugged into the resurrection of Christ.

The Israelites of that day always thought that the Day of the Lord was something that was going to happen in the future. And our culture isn't so much different.

But look at Hebrews 2:8-9

> *In putting everything under him, God left nothing that is not subject to him. Yet at present we do not see everything subject to him. But we see Jesus, who was made a little lower than the angels, now crowned with glory and honor because he suffered*

death, so that by the grace of God he might taste death for everyone.

Now two important phrases from that passage: *Yest at Present* and *But we see Jesus.* They are important because the early church believed that what God did in the body of Jesus is what He was going to do for all of us... for all of creation. Even though at present, we don't see it.

The resurrection meant that evil would never have the final word.

Many centuries ago, a man named Dionysius the Insignificant *(who was a bit bummed about his last name)* came up with the idea to divide history between 2 periods: before Christ and after. And it stuck.

Now every date we write on a check subtly reminds us that a day is coming that the way things are now isn't the way things have to be. Every tombstone in its own way points to a day when they will no longer be needed.

The resurrection explains why in all of history

there is no other phenomenon like the church. The resurrection isn't some doctrine founded by the church. It's the reality that the church founded herself upon. Because without out it, everyday normal people don't stand up to the powers Caesar with nothing but a cross on their backs.

The resurrection means nothing is irreversible.

There is so much more I could say, and I will in the next chapter, but I want to leave you for now with a story of the Kingdom.

Matthew is a child who lives at a children's home close to where I live. He has been so terribly abused physically and sexually that he has to be heavily medicated in order for him to fall asleep and sleep through the night...

Until recently.

Some young people at a local church have recently started going to the home to visit Matthew. And what they have found is that if they will sing lullabies to him before he goes to bed,

Matthew will get a good night's sleep through the night without needing medication.

Can I say something?

I think the Kingdom of Heaven looks a bit more like an abused kid being able to sleep through the night than streets and rivers of gold.

It won't always be this way

Application: What is God telling me?

Heaven Waits

Is that all you've got?

This is the conclusion of the Heaven Waits.

In the previous chapters, I talked about the Day of the Lord or the Day of Judgment, how it applies to the resurrection and what the resurrection meant to the Israelites. We talked about how the Day of Judgment was actually a good thing, and that the resurrection in Christ to the early church, pointed toward the resurrection of the saints, the Day of the Lord, when Christ would resurrect His people, He would make everything right, that things were never irreversible again. We talked about how the Kingdom of God was very much at present to the early church, though it hadn't yet come about.

But in this chapter, I would like to pose a question:

Why did God roll the stone away after the resurrection?

We find out later that Jesus can walk through things, so He didn't need God to roll the stone away. Maybe it was so that the disciples would know for sure that Christ wasn't in the grave, but even this didn't seal their faith. I think there is a different reason. But I'll get back to this a bit later...

I played basketball when I was younger *(and in better shape)*. And though I thought I was much better than I was, I got my fair share of playing time. And very common to basketball is trash talking like...

> *"My grandma has a better jump shot that you do, and she's in a wheelchair!"* or
>
> *"You'll be on my next poster!"*

But possibly the worst thing anyone can say when trash talking is:

> *Is that all you've got?*

This is why that phrase is so belittling... If you give all of your effort and I'm still standing, then eventually you lose. If I give everything and it doesn't defeat you, then eventually you win.

And this is why Paul writes this:

> *But let me tell you something wonderful, a mystery I'll probably never fully understand. We're not all going to die—but we are all going to be changed. You hear a blast to end all blasts from a trumpet, and in the time that you look up and blink your eyes—it's over. On signal from that trumpet from heaven, the dead will be up and out of their graves, beyond the reach of death, never to die again. At the same moment and in the same way, we'll all be changed. In the resurrection scheme of things, this has to happen: everything perishable taken off the shelves and replaced by the imperishable, the mortal replaced by the immortal. Then the saying will come true:*
>
> *Death swallowed by triumphant Life!*
> *Who got the last word, oh, Death?*
> *Oh, Death, who's afraid of you now?*
> *It was sin that made death so frightening and law-code guilt that gave sin its leverage, its destructive power. But now in a single victorious*

stroke of Life, all three—sin, guilt, death—are gone, the gift of our Master, Jesus Christ. Thank God! - I Corinthians 15:54-57

The passage is saying that one day death will not win. That it won't even have a say at all. That in the end evil doesn't win one bit.

Do you want to know why I believe that God rolled the stone away? I don't think the stone was really the point at all. It was what was on the stone.

Around the stone was a ribbon and on that ribbon was a stamp. It was a seal, the mark of Caesar. And breaking this seal was a capital offense against Rome *punishable by death.*

And God broke the seal!

Because what was Caesar to do? Kill him? He already tried that, and Christ resurrected!

I believe the stone being rolled away is God's way of saying to Caesar and ultimately to Satan,

"IS THAT ALL YOU'VE GOT? You tried your best, and I'm still standing."

The early church got this. This is why there has been no phenomenon in history like the church. They took on the powers of Caesar, the Pharisees and ultimately Satan, with fearlessness, without abandon. Because what was Caesar to do? Kill them? Even then, they still win.

But read the passage following the one we just read:

> *With all this going for us, my dear, dear friends, stand your ground. And don't hold back. Throw yourselves into the work of the Master, confident that nothing you do for him is a waste of time or effort.* - I Corinthians 15:58

Paul is talking about working toward the Kingdom of God in knowing that death eventually will be no more. Tied into the Kingdom of God and the resurrection is the idea that we have a big part in it. That we aren't spectators, but partners with God in bringing the Kingdom about.

I used to think that what it meant to be a Christian was to have my sins forgiven, then wait until I died and then go off to some place in the sky that had nothing to do with the world that I live in. And I don't think it was all that different from how many Christians believe today. But Paul seems to think that our role has something to do with the Resurrection or the Kingdom of God.

And they didn't do this for Heaven. They did this for the Kingdom. Not for some place that they would go some day when they died. They didn't wait. They worked, not because it was what was required of them, but because the resurrection meant that the world could be a better place, the kingdom was progressing, God was pulling them forward, and they were called to be partners in the new thing God was doing.

In 1992, a 16 year civil war ended in Mozambique. Though the war ended, there was still a cold war atmosphere in which each tribe stored up their weapons in preparation for the next civil war.

Then came the Christians.

The Christian Relief Aid promised the Mozambique tribes that if they would give up their weapons, they would in exchange receive farm equipment. And the crazy thing is... the tribes agreed.

Tribes were getting tractors and plows and outrageous amounts of tools. But the Christian Relief Aid was then faced with a dilemma. They had all of these weapons, and nothing to do with them. And what they did was clever.

They decided to make a sculpture, out of the weapons traded for farm equipment.

God tells Isaiah about stuff like this at the Day of the Lord:

> *He will judge between the nations*
> *and will settle disputes for many peoples.*
> *They will beat their swords into plowshares*
> *and their spears into pruning hooks.*
> *Nation will not take up sword against nation,*
> *nor will they train for war anymore.*
> - Isaiah 2:4

But best of all... do you know what the Christians named sculpture? The *Tree of Life.*

A group of Christians decided that things shouldn't be this way... that in the Kingdom there was to be no war, and therefore, their role was to partner with God to make this world look a bit more like that world.

This is the Kingdom of God, and this is the call of God for His people. Being a follower of Christ isn't waiting for Heaven. It's partnering with Heaven in bringing the Day of the Lord to earth.

Doomsday Christians go on and on about how this world is just going to get worse. It almost sounds like an excuse to pack our bags and get the heck out of here.

Can I say that I choose to believe differently?

Can I say that I choose to believe that I can make a difference... that *we* can make a difference?

And not only can we, it's our calling. It's who God has called us to be. It's why we are here.

My purpose for living used to be to get married, have a family, make a six figure income, live a good life, then die and go to heaven.

But can I say something?

My reason now for living is the child prostitute. It's little Matthew who must be so heavily medicated in order to sleep at night, due to all of the abuse he has received. It's nations like Mozambique, who are war ravaged, rebuilding and poor. It's those who *NEED* what and Who we take advantage of everyday.

Sure... there may come a day when I leave this world in transition for the Kingdom to come, but know this.

I won't go silently,

Because Heaven waits.

Is that all you've got?

Application: What is God telling me?

The Author

Josh Bruckerhoff is a Christian, husband, father, son, brother and friend. He resides in Dallas, Texas. Josh holds a degree in Church Ministries and has served as both Worship and Youth Minister, in addition to teaching ministry classes and leading small groups. Josh has a unique style of delivering the message of Christ in a way that is relevant and applicable to everyone who hears it. He believes that being a Christian is not a destination, but a journey; and he respects the fact that all believers aren't at the same place in that journey. His message is one that is tailored to people where they are in life.

Josh has a passion for seeing others live up to their full potential in Christ. He desires that people realize the gifts that God has put inside of them so that they can share them to enrich the lives of others. Understanding that God doesn't live in our world, but that we live in His, Josh encourages others to share Christ, not only in words, but in relationships.

Josh enjoys sharing his thoughts and experiences on his website: www.thekidtheking.com.

For more information, he can be contacted at Josh@thekidtheking.com

www.ingramcontent.com/pod-product-compliance
Ingram Content Group UK Ltd.
Pitfield, Milton Keynes, MK11 3LW, UK
UKHW020215250726
13967UKWH00001B/9

9 781300 921479